Christian Prepping 101: How To Start Prepping

By: Tom Eckerd

Special Request

Thank you for purchasing our book and supporting our Ministry. We have a Special Request for those that have purchased this book on the Kindle platform. We wanted to make you aware that Amazon's Kindle platform pays per pages "read". Our Special Request is that if you appreciate our Ministry's efforts to put out books such as this or if you would simply like to support our Ministry's work to please scroll to the back of the book, even if you don't "read" the book right away. This is how we will get paid through the paid per pages criteria.

We all lead such busy lives nowadays and can get side tracked so easily please take a moment to support us now by allowing us to be paid by scrolling to the end of the book – Then go back and read it at your leisure.

We deeply appreciate Your support and know that God will Bless You as You have Blessed this Ministry.

Table of Contents

Special Request...3

Dedication 6

Forward 7

Chapter 1: What is Christian Prepping............9

Chapter 2: Understand the Why...................16

Chapter 3: Spiritual Survival........................22

Chapter 4: What is God's Plan......................26

Chapter 5: Educating Yourself 29

Chapter 6: Five Foundations of Survival 33

Chapter 7: How to Start Prepping.................53

Chapter 8: Kits & Bags..................................81

Chapter 9: The EDC 86

Chapter 10: The Bug Out Bag 91

Chapter 11: The INCH Bag 96

Chapter 12: The Bug Out Vehicle (BOV)......101

Chapter 13: The Bug Out Retreat (BOR)......105

Chapter 14: Caching 108

Chapter 15: Alternative Housing Options ...114

Chapter 16: Alternative Energy Options 116

Chapter 17: What to Buy.............................120

Chapter 18: Personal Care..........................124

Conclusion 127

Special Gift...129

Stay In Contact.......................................131

Find All Our Books On Amazon...................132

Dedication

This book is dedicated to the watchmen of God who faithfully watch and pray as Lord commanded all of us to do and to my Lord and Savior Jesus Christ who continues to lead, guide and protect us as we move forward in courage and faith to shine the light into the darkness.

Forward

This book is a follow-up to our previous book, Biblical Bug Out: Don't Bug In - Follow The Calling. In the previous book we discussed the concept of bugging out and indicated through Scripture how this was a Biblical principle. We felt compelled in our spirit, given the lateness of the hour to put out that book first to provide immediate solutions to Christians looking for answers in dark times.

In this book we laid the foundations of what we consider to be "Christian Prepping". If you're a Christian and into prepping you should enjoy this book as a gives a clear concise systematic approach to prepping from a Christian perspective. We have attempted to touch on all of the critical items one should consider when seeking to be prepared. For many Christian Preppers just starting out this may in fact end up being your go to book as you prepare you and your family for what's to come.

Preppers in general have many reasons for preparing - Some see economic collapse on the horizon, some see an EMP detonated over the United States knocking on the power grid, others may see cyber terrorism infecting the majority of computers and infrastructure of the United States, still yet others may see a World War III scenario taking place - Preppers have so many things they are preparing for. However, the Christian Prepper may have less to consider or more to consider depending upon how you look at things. One thing is for certain the Christian Prepper is unique within the prepping community as their focus for it centers on Jesus Christ and the events leading to His imminent return.

Start your journey now by reading this book and gaining necessary insight on how you and your family can be truly prepared.

Chapter 1: What is Christian Prepping

What is Christian prepping some might ask. Christian prepping can be defined as prepping based off of prophecy and the Word of God. In the Word of God we can find many examples of various men and women of faith who God warned of things to come and enabled them to prepare. In today's modern times God still operates the same way, He still warns his people of the dangers to come – both physical dangers as well spiritual dangers. Christian prepping combines both aspects to enable the believer to prepare fully for what's to come.

One of the fundamental differences of Christian prepping versus just prepping is that Christian prepping is centered around a belief, a passion and a sincere desire to put Jesus Christ first and foremost in everything we do – it is the fact that we prep not out of fear of what is to come or what may come but a genuine love for our families and those around us - knowing that in a time of need, a time of crisis we must stand in the gap and be prepared.

For the Christian Prepper their greatest prep, their greatest asset rather is the Holy Spirit, the Word of God and as I mentioned before Jesus Christ. To the Christian Prepper it's not about stuff that we may acquire to deal with a particular situation or scenario. Having these things are great but if you don't have Christ, if you are not spiritually prepared to die at this very moment then none of that matters. No amount of stuff, no amount of gear, no amount of ammo or food or water can ever take the place of the living water of Jesus Christ that He will give you – and it is this living water that sustains us - the Word of God and the precious Holy Spirit.

Christian prepping most likely is centered, for most believers, around End Time theology. In the last days the Bible indicates that Christians will be hated throughout all of the world for Jesus Christ namesake, it indicates also in the book of Daniel that our enemy will prevail against us physically until Christ returns and judgment is made in favor of His saints. In the book of Revelation of Jesus Christ we read also that Christians will be hunted down and martyred for their testimony of Our Lord Jesus Christ and the faith they hold near to heart.

So as you can read for the Christian there is much to prepare for, yet nothing we can do can stop what is written - for what is written will come to pass regardless. Embrace it, plan for it, and mitigate your families suffering if possible through God's grace.

To further clarify, the Bible indicates that there are three that make war against us as Christians in these last days - the Antichrist, the Beast, and the Dragon that old serpent of old.

It may seem overwhelming and a pointless endeavor to even consider prepping but God did not leave us alone – He gave His Holy Spirit to us, and In 1 John 4:4 We read the Greater is He that is in us then he that is in the World.

What an awesome God we serve, giving us mercy and grace when we sin and repent, giving us the wisdom and the awareness through His Word and through the Spirit of revelation to understand what's coming and to prepare for. He didn't leave us helpless by any means of the imagination. We each have the power and authority Christ has given us through His Holy Spirit – use it.

So how does the Christian prep or prepare for these things that must come to pass - Well for starters you have to be in excellent spiritual fitness. The Bible declares that in these last days that men's hearts would fail them for the fear of the knowledge of what is to come. We as Christian Preppers must learn to build up our courage and faith in Christ to proclaim boldly the Word of God - for it is the power of God unto Salvation. Knowing who you are in Christ and what your enemy's tactics are is the key – Understand Your authority in Christ!!

You know my question to you is this, if you had one opportunity, one last opportunity to speak to someone that you love before eternity came and took them away - what would you say? God has given us this very situation right now, in all honesty that's one of the reasons this book is being created, to reach out one last time before eternity is an ever present reality. This physical life has eternal consequences - one way or another after you die you will either go to heaven or you will go to hell, but there is no second chance once you're in eternity.

If you're a Prepper but not a Christian Prepper I would ask you one question – why are you prepping in the first place? Is it to save your life, your family's life, take back the country from out-of-control politicians? My assumption is that you are preparing because you wish to survive whatever scenario you see in the future or currently and if you have a family, I think I can say with relative confidence that you prepare so you can save their lives as well.

But understand this Mr. & Mrs. Prepper without Jesus Christ you fall short in your preps and your family, your love ones, your friends, and you will not survive. If you're serious about preparing then you must prepare in every aspect of one's life. Leaving out the most critical portion of your preparations is not intelligent and will surely leave you without hope, leave you without peace, and leave you without confidence.

Because without the Spirit of God dwelling in you, without Jesus Christ in your heart, you will not have that living water I spoke of earlier to refresh and center you – Jesus Christ is the well and without Him it's nothing but a desert.

Without Jesus Christ you will be driven mad by fear, uncertainty, and all the "What If's" that are in your mind. However, with Jesus Christ in your heart as your personal Lord and Savior you will have a peace, confidence, and boldness to do what must be done.

Now there's no way in a small little book like this that I can reach out to you the way that I truly want to and reason with you and encourage you to come to the knowledge of the truth in Christ Jesus before it is too late. If you think your gonna survive whatever may happen, whatever's going on – you may, but what if you don't? Wouldn't you want to have the certainty of everlasting life for you and your family – this is a serious question and there is no way to express my heartfelt sincerity with mere words but I implore you as best I can in the love of God, and the love of Jesus Christ come to Him now because tomorrow is not guaranteed. I will leave some further insight at the end of this book if you are seriously considering opening your heart to Jesus Christ and getting right with God. I hope that you will check out the special gift in the back of the book to help guide you along the path to getting right with God.

If you do become a born-again Christian I want to hear from you - I want you to come to our website, is pretty easy to find, it's located in this book and throughout the web. I want you to drop me a line and reach out to me because I want to join with you in a real and personal way and help you mature in Christ through teaching you proper doctrine. The door is always open I will never force anything on you but I will tell you straight, openly and honestly with the love of Christ the truth to the best of my ability. I hope you will take that step of faith and consider these words and truly join the family of God – I look forward to hearing from you soon.

"Spiritual Preparedness Always Comes Before Physical Preparedness that is the fundamental principle to remember about Christian Prepping" – AJF 03/21/2016 9:28pm

Chapter 2: Understand the Why

To understand the why is to understand all of prophecy. To understand the why is to be granted a Spirit of Revelation – for without the Spirit of Revelation no man can understand the why. For many Christians Preppers the why may be already innately within them from the Word of God and the Spirit of God bringing to remembrance those words.

What do we read in the Scriptures? We read about the Four Horsemen of the Apocalypse, we read about wars and rumors of wars, we read about famine and pestilence, earthquakes - we read about the beginning of sorrows in Matthew 24. In Matthew 24 it also talks about the fact that for Jesus Christ namesake, for our testimony, for our faith we will be hated in all of the world. My question to you the Christian Prepper is do you understand what happens after they hate us, after the label us, after they begin to discriminate against us and our faith?

If you're a brother or sister in Christ rightly dividing the Word of God you understand what comes next. They will set up and succeed at bringing in the Mark the Beast in Revelations 13:16, 17 - at which point the Christians will be backed into a corner in which they will not be able to buy or sell anything. Combine that with the fact that the entire world hates us and is discriminating against us – what is the logical and reasonable thing to do in such a situation - for certainly they will come, they will come in the night, they will come just like they came for Jesus in the night or the Jews, to round us up and to kill us. This is just what our enemy does.

But God in his mercy has given us the wisdom and the awareness to see the things that the world is blind to and to prepare accordingly. However, understand this - how the Christian prepares is massively different than how the average Prepper prepares.

So going back to the original question – why? The why is simple – God commands us to provide and to protect our families, He provides examples throughout the Old and New Testament of this very thing.

Whether it's an Ark, whether it's in the Lions Den, or whether it's during the tribulation God's always is in control and provides a way of escape for His people according to His will and the faith of His people.

Many people who call themselves Christians that believe in what they label a pre-tribulation rapture believe that God will supernaturally come back prior to any tribulation so they will not have to endure anything. However that is a false teaching, it is not Biblically sound – the same people most likely will be the ones in the great falling away.

God never said that He would rescue us from Tribulation; He said that we are not appointed to wrath. Jesus also spoke through Paul and indicated that we must endure hardship as a good soldier of Jesus Christ - what is hardship but tribulation.

The point here I'm trying to make is very simple to those that follow Christ, those that truly follow Christ they will have to endure the seals of God which is the tribulation but even through that God will provide for His people. Many of us will be martyred during this time in the 5th Seal, this is what's written, this is what must come to pass.

However at the same time I challenge believers out there, my brothers and sisters in Christ to consider the possibilities of preparing now to mitigate the amount of suffering that your family may have to endure. The Bible declares that God's people perish for lack of knowledge. So what does that mean to the Christian Prepper – it means that the more we are prepared both with knowledge and wisdom the more we stand a better chance not to parish for lacking it.

The choice of course is always yours whether to ignore warnings such as this and this book, warnings found in the Bible itself, or warnings deep within your spirit that are dropped there by the Holy Spirit – There're consequences for things that you do and their consequences for things that you do not do. I don't want to sound in such a way as to cause fear within your heart because the things that I speak and write to you today I speak in love encouraging you to get prepared and follow the examples that we have written ever so clearly in the Word of God.

My goal here is to put a sense of urgency within your heart and provide solutions as God enables through this book to deal systematically with helping you prepare to an adequate level in which you can fulfill the call of God on your life.

Verses to Consider to Be Prepared as the Lord directs us:

Luke: 22: 35-38: (35) And He said to them, "When I sent you without money bag, knapsack, and sandals, did you lack anything?" so they said, "Nothing." (36) Then He said to them, "But now, he who has a money bag, let him take it, and likewise a knapsack; and he who has no sword, let him sell his garment and buy one. (37) For I say to you that this which is written must still be accomplished in Me: 'And He was numbered with the transgressors. For the things concerning Me have an end." (38) So they said, "Lord, look, here are two swords." And He said to them, "It is enough."

Understanding God's Purpose and Plan
During these Times

2 Timothy 2:3 - 3 You therefore must endure
hardship as a good soldier of Jesus Christ.

Luke 21:12 But before all these things, they
will lay their hands on you and persecute
you, delivering you up to the synagogues and
prisons. You will be brought before kings and
rulers for My name's sake. (13) But it will
turn out for you as an occasion for testimony.
(14) Therefore settle it in your hearts not to
meditate beforehand on what you will
answer; (15) for I will give you a mouth and
wisdom which all your adversaries will not
be able to contradict or resist. (16) You will
be betrayed even by parents and brothers,
relatives and friends; and they will put some
of you to death. (17) And you will be hated
by all for My name's sake. (18) But not a hair
of your head shall be lost. (19) By your
patience possess your souls.

Chapter 3: Spiritual Survival

Understanding Spiritual Survival from a Christian perspective may be a little challenging at first glance. A sizable percentage of the prepping and survival community may consider themselves to be Christian; yet all too often, we talk about our survival plans as if God had nothing to do with them. Yet nothing could be farther from the truth. Without God's help and intervention, none of us have much of a chance of surviving anything – not even if we Bug Out.

Truly, we must be dependent upon God. But that dependence needs to start long before a disaster hits. If we expect to live by faith in the midst of a crisis and haven't been living by faith in our day-to-day lives, we are going to fail miserably. Learning to live by faith requires time and practice. It also requires going through the hard times, so that you can become accustomed to leaning on the Lord in the midst of them.

Any survival planning you do must include the Lord. That's where Spiritual Survival needs to start. You and I both need the guidance of the Holy Spirit to decide on everything from the right amount of gear, to the right place to Bug Out to. Trying to do these things in our own strength or knowledge puts us at a distinct disadvantage and in the same boat as those in the world; as if we didn't have God's help readily available to us.

There's more to Spiritual Survival than just asking God to help us make the right plans. To be honest, the average Christian today is spiritually lazy. We expect a pastor to do everything for us, rather than thinking for ourselves and doing what God calls us to do ourselves. But what are we going to do when that pastor isn't there? Have you made plans to bring your pastor along as part of your Spiritual Survival plan? Do you have enough supplies to feed him and his family too?

One of the beauties of the New Testament is the priesthood of the believer. We don't need a pastor or priest between God, and ourselves because we already have one in Jesus Christ.

Jesus, in His role as the High Priest, intercedes for us continually before the Father. So, while a pastor maybe useful (If they're not working as part of the clergy response teams), they are not a requirement for us to find and depend on God.

However, few believers are truly prepared to encounter God on their own. We are a nation of spiritual babies, expecting our pastors to change our diapers and give us our bottles. That won't get us through a survival situation and enable Spiritual Survival. We're going to have to know the Word of God to understand how to stand on our own two feet, as well as how to pastor others.

When a disaster or significant persecution arises, we're going to have to be ready to spiritually care for our families. The Bible you bring will be the only "pastor" you have. And if you lose your Bible – You're going to need to know the Bible; know how to teach it and know how to live it. We're also going to have to know how to give counsel from it; pray for our families when they are sick and witness to those we encounter. Discipleship is the Great Commission but it starts in our own home first.

You will need to be prepared to feed your family spiritually, so that their faith can remain steadfast and strong. Regular family Bible studies or even home church services will need to become part of your Spiritual Survival plan. If you've never experienced God in the middle of a meadow in the mountains, you're missing out. Some of the greatest spiritual experiences of your life may very well happen after you Bug Out and are dependent on God.

To do that, we need to prepare ourselves today; otherwise, we won't be ready for the life we are going to live tomorrow. If you are not a serious student of the Word of God, then I've got to say that you aren't ready right now. You're still expecting someone else to do it for you; and as long as you're doing that, you're not going to know how to count on God, when things go bad.

Chapter 4: What is God's Plan

If you still reading here in chapter 4 I commend your dedication as most people pick up a book and never get past the second chapter, for that alone I commend your dedication. Let's now discuss God's plan for these dark times. There are countless examples throughout history and throughout the Bible of God commanding his people to bug out. I won't go too much in depth or give too many examples in this particular section if you would like more in-depth look at bugging out from a biblical perspective I encourage you to read our book Biblical Bug Out: Don't Bug In - Follow The Calling. Yes that is a selfish plug for our book but I do feel that this book can help fast-track anyone who is a believer in Jesus Christ get a firm understanding of bugging out and why it's so critical to plan for that. Nevertheless let us continue. Escape and Evasion, this is a military term that has to do with eluding one's enemy during a military conflict. This is the very principle God has directed us to use during these dark times.

Let's examine a Scripture verse:

God says flee to the mountains and don't go back to get anything – therefore, watch and pray and be ready at all times – Matt. 24:15-20 / Mark 13

Mark 13: 14 -19 [14 "So when you see the 'abomination of desolation, spoken of by Daniel the prophet, standing where it ought not" (let the reader understand), "then let those who are in Judea flee to the mountains. (15) Let him who is on the housetop not go down into the house, nor enter to take anything out of his house. (16) And let him who is in the field not go back to get his clothes. (17) But woe to those who are pregnant and to those who are nursing babies in those days! (18) And pray that your flight may not be in winter. (19) For in those days there will be tribulation, such as has not been since the beginning of the creation which God created until this time, nor ever shall be.]

Now the abomination of desolation spoken of by the prophet Daniel what does this truly mean. If you read the King James Version that uses the terminology "It".

I propose a question at this time, has the abomination of desolation already taken place? A third temple has been rebuilt - "it" stands in Brazil. Any Christian or even any Jew for that matter understands that Solomon's Temple is not supposed to be in Brazil.

This is debatable of course and they're many that would say this or that but one thing is for certain a third Temple has been built. That fact alone should give cause to many to evaluate and research if the abomination of desolation has already taken place or may be about to happen. This third Temple was built to exact specifications of the original one with material imported from Israel and the Middle East. A quick search online will reveal all the information one would need.

I've heard rumors for years about secret plans that the Jews in Israel have for rebuilding a third Temple I'm not sure of the accuracy of these reports but as I mentioned a third Temple has already been built and it stands in Brazil.

Chapter 5: Educating Yourself

Educating yourself is like investing in yourself and your family for the future. The more that you educate yourself on things like being prepared, survival, and spiritual warfare the better off you and your family will be. Nowadays college students can spend anywhere from $30,000.00 to $150,000.00 for a college education - whether it's a lawyer, teacher, or doctor Though these professions may have certain values to them, if you were any one of those people in those particular professions in the middle of the woods or middle of the forest would you be able to survive?

If your profession that you spent thousands of dollars educating yourself on is pointless when it comes to actual physical survival skills you need to educate yourself now. If you were willing to spend thousands of dollars on a college education that honestly isn't worth that much nowadays and will not prepare you or your family to survive in the middle of nowhere you got to ask yourself what is the point. Now what would happen if you invested the same amount of money you spent to go to college on being prepared?

I believe that the Native American Indians had it right - everyone was trained in particular skills that enabled them to live off of the land in a harmonious type of way without destroying it but living in balance. If you spent thousands of dollars on a skill, on a trade, or on a degree and you don't have the skills necessary still to survive off the land it's time to reinvest in educating yourself and gain these viable lifesaving skills.

Now thankfully God in His mercy and grace has enabled you to learn through books like this whether online or physically. Additionally with the advent of the Internet and companies like You Tube there is a tremendous amount of resources available free of charge or with books like this at a minimum cost. The amount of value that you can get from one awesome book or one great video that can literally give you the skills to save you or your family member's life – how can you honestly put a price tag on that? It's like asking how much is your life worth, how much is your family's life worth – thankfully most of these skills can be picked up by investing more time than money.

I would encourage every brother and sister out there to get a small collection of books that they're actually going to read as well as some small manuals with specific detailed information that you put in your bug out bag just in case you forget a particular skill to have the book as a resource. In fact I would say every bug out bag should probably have two books at least in them, a King James Version Bible and a survival manual.

In addition to small group of books I would also encourage you to create a You Tube account and learn how to develop play list. Then start adding videos to your playlist that teach you solid information on key areas like shelter building, water purification, fire building, knife selection, etc.

All of this education is great but much like your gear if you don't test it out prior to needing it you're not going to know if it works and you may be up that proverbial river without a paddle. It's absolutely critical to get out on whatever land you plan to survive on and test the skills that you have acquired through reading and observing – it's what we call "Dirt Time".

After reading and observing the next logical step is doing, practicing the knowledge that you have learned. Thus after practicing that knowledge turns into wisdom and that wisdom turns into practical application of learned skills. The American Christian Defense Alliance, Inc. outdoor ministry of the Burning Bush Survival and Preparedness School is currently also in the development of various courses to help prepare you. Please visit our website and sign up for a mailing list for future updates.

Chapter 6: Five Foundations of Survival

Selecting a Survival Knife

Of all your survival equipment, the single most important piece (besides your Bible) is a good knife. Many experts have agreed that if they had to pick only one piece of equipment to use, it would be their knife. That makes sense really, as you can make much of the rest of what you need out of what nature provides you, if you have a knife to work with. No other single piece of equipment does more.

The question then becomes, what sort of knife should you buy? There are a plethora of knives available on the market, available for a wide range of prices and with a large range of options to choose from. There are even knives marketed as survival knives, which contain all sorts of extra equipment to help you survive. So, what's the best?

First of all, this is one place where quality counts more than anything else. If you are going to depend on a knife to help you survive, you need one that is going to hold up under the strain of heavy use, without a risk of it breaking and hopefully with the ability to maintain a good, sharp edge.

With that being our criteria, the first thing to consider is the knife's construction. You want a fixed-blade knife, rather than a folding one. Folding knives can break more easily and the lock can slip at an inopportune moment, causing a serious injury. A folding knife is fine as a backup, but your primary knife should be fixed-blade.

The blade needs to have a full tang. This refers to the part of the blade that extends back through the handle. Manufacturers of cheap knives use partial tangs to save money. But the handle is likely to break right at the end of the tang, when the knife is subject to extreme pressure, leaving you with a blade that doesn't have a handle. That's awfully hard to work with.

I would recommend a blade style that gives you a strong point, as the point is the most fragile part of the blade. Drop point knives are pretty good for this, as well as tonto blades. I personally like clip point knives a lot, because you get a sharper point; but those are not as good for survival knives. The same can be said for dagger point knives. Besides, you don't need a fighting knife as a survival knife, you need a working tool.

The other main issue is the steel that the knife is made of. Most commercially made knives today are made of some sort of stainless steel. That is nice in that it doesn't rust, but stainless steel doesn't hold an edge like high-carbon steel does. The best knives have been made of high-carbon steel for centuries.

Some of the best high-carbon steel comes out of Solingen, Germany. This town is known for their knives, most of which are kitchen knives. However, there are a few companies in Solingen who produce outdoor knives. Just make sure you're actually getting one made in Solingen, and not a cheap knock-off.

Another very popular option is true Damascus steel. This is actually a layered laminate of high-carbon steel and a softer spring steel. The two together provide an excellent edge, while keeping the knife from becoming brittle. High-carbon steel by itself is so hard, that it can be brittle at times. Damascus steel is the one truly obvious steel option, because its layers cause a striped pattern in the knife's blade.

But other than Damascus steel, it's very hard to tell the difference between other types of steel. Not all manufacturers will give you that information, essentially expecting you to trust them for the selection of a good steel for your knife.

There are a number of companies who produce excellent knives. It seems that each survival expert has their favorite. ESSE, Tops, Cold Steel, and Becker are popular brands, all three of which specialize in survival and combat knives. The old standbys of K-Bar and Gerber are good choices as well; especially for people who don't want to spend as much money.

Whatever brand you ultimately choose, realize that you're not going to get a quality knife at a bargain basement price. Cheap knives are just that... cheap. Most especially, they use cheap steel, which won't hold an edge. To get a good knife, you're going to have to spend some money; somewhere between $70 and $200.

Avoid knives with a built-in saw blade, unless the saw blade is on the back side of the knife. A two inch long saw blade isn't going to accomplish much for you and it's going to shorten the knife's effective blade, reducing what you can do with it. You should also avoid "gimmick" knives, which are selling you a survival kit in a knife. Remember, to give you the other stuff, they have to reduce the cost of the knife. That's done by using cheaper steel.

Shelter

Regardless of whether you're trying to make your way home after a disaster, trying to bug out after a disaster, or just trying to make your way out after being lost in the wilderness, shelter is going to be an important factor.

Shelter is one of the things we use to protect ourselves from the weather and maintain our body heat, making it one of our most important survival priorities.

The biggest killer in the wild is hypothermia, the loss of body heat. This can happen year-round, as the ambient air temperature is normally lower than our body's temperature. When we get wet, either through excessive sweating, rain or from falling in a body of water, our bodies shed heat rapidly. Without shelter, it doesn't take long for hypothermia to set in.

That's why it's important to always carry some sort of shelter materials in your bug out bag or EDC bag (everyday carry bag). It doesn't take much; you don't need an expensive backpacking tent. A simple tarp and some cordage will help you make a descent shelter in a pinch.

But more important than the materials you are carrying is to start with what nature offers. There are a lot of things that can be used for shelter, when in the wild. Some can be used as they are, while others may need to be improved with the help of your tarp and cordage. Either way, starting with what nature provides makes the job easier.

So, what sorts of things can you look for in nature to use as shelter? Caves – Check to make sure they are unoccupied, before going in. Rock Outcroppings – They will often have places where two or three rocks have a space between them which can quickly be converted to a cave. Undercut Embankments – Rivers or flash floods can undercut an embankment, creating a wide but shallow cave. With a wind screen in front and a fire in-between, this makes a comfortable shelter.

Overturned Trees – The space below the tree can be cleaned out for a shelter or the root mass makes a good back wall for a shelter. Thickets of Trees – Often saplings will grow close enough together to create a hidden spot which blocks off the wind.

You might have to cut a few saplings out of the middle and string your tarp overhead, but it will provide a great windbreak. Other than the caves, you'll have to make some modifications in pretty much all these cases.

That's where your tarp and cordage come in. The tarp can either be used as a roof or as walls, depending on the needs of your particular shelter.

Another great material that you can find in the wild is to use tree branches. Layered against the side of the shelter or on the roof, they shed rain well and provide good resistance to break up the wind.

The key here, more than anything, is being able to improvise. Simply opening your eyes and seeing what nature has already created is the first step in creating any shelter. Then, it's just a matter of figuring out how to make that shelter more rain and wind proof, as well as where you can place your fire to keep you warm.

Fire

Fire has to be one of the most useful tools that God has given mankind. While our main use of fire is to help keep us warm, it goes beyond that in meeting our needs. Fire also provides us with light, a means of cooking our food and even a way of purifying water. All this makes fire an essential for survival. While we could theoretically survive without it, trying to do so requires much more effort than building and maintaining the fire does. So, it ultimately makes more sense to have a fire as a part of any survival effort, than not to have it. Actually, it's one of the first things we should do.

If you've ever watched someone try to start a fire, who doesn't know what they're doing, you should have a pretty good appreciation of the difficulty involved. If we were to analyze the fire starting methodology of these people, we'd probably quickly encounter that they are causing much of their own problem. Most specifically, they aren't working their way up through the different types of flammable materials correctly.

What do I mean by that? I mean starting with tinder, working your way up to kindling and then to the fuel for your fire. Most of the time, they try to jump from tinder to fuel or sometimes from a match to fuel. What's the difference between these things? Tinder consists of things that will catch fire easily from one match or other fire starter. You can include dry grass, newspaper, char-cloth, dryer lint and dry moss in this category. Every fire needs tinder to get it started. Kindling is small flammable material that will burn longer than the rapid-burning tinder and allow the flame to grow so that it will ultimately catch the fuel on fire. Usually, we're talking about sticks the diameter of your finger here. Larger sticks can be used, if they are made into a "fuzz stick."

Fuel is what your fire is going to burn to provide you with heat. Typically, we're talking about pieces about the diameter of your arm. This gives a nice balance between catching fire fairly easily and not burning too quickly. About the only time you want chunks of wood larger than this, is if you are setting the fire up to burn through the night.

These three types of material need to be set up in a teepee or pyramid structure, so that the burning tinder can catch the kindling on fire and then the kindling can catch the fuel on fire. As flame, like any other heat rises, this is typically done by putting the tinder on the bottom, with the kindling above it and the fuel forming the outer shell.

There are many ways you can provide an initial spark, ember or flame to the fuel, in order to start a fire. Survival instructors collect fire starting methods like some people collect baseball cards. But if you have simple fire starters, you might want to use them. This usually means waterproof matches or a butane lighter.

A lighter is probably the best single fire starter you can carry. A typical lighter will start about 1,000 fires, if it is used carefully and not wasted. It's compact, fairly water resistant and reliable. The only problem is that it won't work in cold weather. But to solve this problem, you can keep the lighter inside your clothing to keep it warm.

Most survival instructors say you should carry two primary and two secondary forms of fire starting. Lighters and matches are the primary means. Things like metal matches, Ferro Rods, magnifying glasses, 0000 steel wool and a battery, and a bow drill all fall into the category. Other than for practice, you really only want to use one of these secondary methods in the case where you don't have your primary methods. I prefer to carry two lighters, one of which is totally waterproof, rather than mess with those other methods (although I have them too).

One other thing you should always carry for starting a fire is an accelerant. This is something, usually chemical, which will burn readily.

While the term "accelerant" is normally used in association with arson, it's the correct term to use in this case as well. If you do a search online for "fire starters" you'll find some of these, along with things like the Metal Match and Ferro Rod. Some of the best are cube shaped and individually wrapped.

A fire accelerant is especially useful when it is wet out. You really don't want to use them all the time, but if it is raining, you'll be glad you have one. You can make your own as well, by working petroleum jelly into cotton balls. One cotton ball, treated in this way, will burn for over three minutes, making it great for getting a stubborn fire started.

Water

Water is one of the key elements to life and survival. During a crisis situation, SHTF, or your Bug Out finding and making potable water is a must. It's important to understand the time frame that your body has for needing water. Your body runs best when properly hydrated each and every day. Lack of hydration will cause lack of focus and lack of focus will cause poor decisions to be made – it's not just physical thing - your body needing water.

Water affects everything. Your body can only survive approximately 3 days without water. That being said it's vital to understand how to find water and how to make it drinkable.

There lots of filters and purifiers on the market today each one having its own unique benefits and disadvantages. Check our website for current recommendations. However, having a steel container to boil water in will go a long way to making water potable.

Now considering that the mentality and the plan that God has for us is to escape and evade we might not be in a position in which fire would be such a good idea. There are lots of ways to hide a fire such as a Dakota fire pit but in all reality sometimes it's better not to take the chance and build a fire while being hunted. You have to remember, even if they can't see your fire they might be able to smell your smoke or see a smoke signal. If you built a fire close to the thick evergreen tree you might be able to hide the smoke for those around but it's still not a good idea while in escape and evade mode.

Therefore, that's when certain water filters water purifiers come in the play. They enable you to have fresh clean drinking potable water without the need of the fire – a significant tactical advantage for you while on the run. Again check our website for the most updated list of recommendations.

When trying to acquire up in the Surrey water for survival as you bug out there a few options. You could attempt to catch water with a tarp or poncho and drain that water into a steel container and boil it. The fire is not an option that you could still drain the water into your container; however, this is where you would need something similar to a Life Straw (which is a lightweight filter that you drink out of).

Another option for the Christian Prepper would be to read the terrain to determine if there is a stream, Creek or other potential body of water in the local vicinity. Obviously all water flows downhill so as you continue to move down there is a greater chance to find water.

This is where being prepared and having foresight comes into play. If you have prepared your bug out bag appropriately prior to needing it you should have your water containers already filled as well as the appropriate necessities to process water appropriately for safe consumption. Another great option is water tabs.

Now for those with a thyroid condition you may want to watch your iodine consumption. However, these are a great option as they are the latest option available and can be thrown into any pocket or kit. Just remember you're still good and need a steel container I cannot over emphasize the importance of the steel container. I should also mention that it's important to have a wide mouth steel container, as this will give you more options and make your life just a little bit easier on the go.

Food

Everything has it's purpose in your systems and Long Term Food Storage is no different. That being said, I would also say that All LTFS is only a backup to other backups you have in place.

You should strive to live a life in which you produce your own food or source it directly from nature - Don't rely on others to feed you, chances are you will no doubt starve at a rapid rate.

Long Term Food Storage should not be confused with food that you utilize in your Bug Out Bag / Go Bag or Bug Out Vehicle or in a Cache'. This is not the intended purpose for LTFS.

For these systems you should consider MREs (Meals Ready to Eat) and Mainstay Food Ration Bars (3600 Cal.). Both also make great additions to any cache and do not require any water to actually cook or produce . . . Unlike the Long Term Food Storage options which will require water to make.

Grab & Go should be just that to limit the amount of extra worry in your food preparations. Furthermore, take time to explore, study, and learn about wild edibles - this knowledge alone could save your life.

Grab & Go Options (No Preparation Needed)
- Self life of 5-7 Years

MREs (Meals Ready-to-Eat)
Mainstay Food Rations (3600 Cal)

LTFS = Long Term Food Storage

There are a lot of options out there for anyone when it comes to Long Term Food Storage (LTFS) including Do It Yourself Options such as canning or vacuum sealing your own food. If your resources and abilities permit it this is the cheapest option to get the most bang for your buck. Yet when you need to Bug Out all that food stays right there unless you have it cached in a safe location. LTFS Companies that offer who have freeze dried food in buckets help with the transportation or transition of such food but it still is in a bucket so you can't bring it when you go on foot.

Now I've done the math here and for some of the LTFS options or plans if you would you could purchase Grab & Go Back Packing Options such as Backpackers Pantry. I recently did just that.

One thing that really gets to me is how the so called LTFS business doesn't include any real meat in their meals - What do you see out there? Pasta, Soups, Rice, Some Beans, and a whole lot of Cheese. I'm not sure about anyone else but I keep thinking of the old Wendy's commercial when they say, "Where the Beef"

99% of the time you have to purchase the meat separately and it's ridiculous in price, so what's another way to move forward with a practical plan that gives you the protein you will need in a stressful situation? Backpackers Pantry or another similar option – and with these when you Bug Out they come with you, well at least some of it – Try that will a 50lbs of Rice, good luck, lol. Also go as organic and healthy as possible - if you put "Crap" in your body you literally will get "Crap" out.

Can goods are another great way to get protein on the cheap, relatively speaking that is. Check out your local wholesale club - We shop at BJs and they are doing a great job moving to more organic items. However, again just remember you're not going to throw a bunch of can goods in your Bug Out Bag, it's just too heavy.

Now I don't want you to walk away thinking that long-term food storage is a waste of time, it's not. You don't know what situations can take place and for that reason alone you should have long-term food storage. The Word of God says no one knows the day or the hour but we are able to read the seasons – that being said is good to plan accordingly. Remember there will be famine throughout the land prior, I repeat prior to us being hated and persecuted and martyred. So to help us endure and whether the storm it's critical to have enough food stored up both at your house and other various locations.

How much food? Well that honestly depends on the size of your family, on how long you desire to feed them - six months, a year, or maybe five years. As a Christian Prepper I would recommend at least four years' worth of food to be stored up if at all financially possible. I would recommend freeze-dried as the best option. Freeze-dried food does carry a higher price point but you are receiving all the nutrients unlike the dehydrated foods.

Long Term Food Storage does have its place in the Christian Preppers life especially if you have a Bug Out Retreat or if you don't plan to Bug Out. For the Christian Prepper who has the resources it would be a great idea to purchase LTFS and Cache it in various places. Keep in mind with any LTFS Company you have to Read the Fine Print and know what to look for. There is an Art and a Science to buying LTFS. Our organization does support some LTFS as an option and is partnering with selected companies that provide the greatest value and benefits to those we serve. Check our website for the latest reviews on companies and their products.

Your stockpile of food for you and your family should consist of a multi layered system where options such as bugging out and bugging in are considered. Additionally, caches of preparations and food along commonly travel routes and approximately 5 miles away from your home should be considered as vital links in your overall survival plan.

Chapter 7: How to Start Prepping

Developing Your Systems & Planning Things Out - Including SOPs

First and foremost you need to understand what the Word of God has to say about preparing, as well as prophecy in these last days. From there it will be important to start to understand how to prepare by reading books like this. After learning how to get things organized and having a basic operational framework for your preparedness objectives learning and practicing survival skills is next up on the to do list.

The following are some considerations to think about to help you develop your systems and SOPs (Standard Operating Procedures) for you and your family. Every Family will have slightly different needs so there was no point in attempting to add a universal plan – something like that does not exist and if it did would most likely have very little real world application for you and your family.

Family Preparedness Plans: Family Rules of Preparedness – Develop Habits to Keep You Alive

Having a clearly understandable Threat Level System is important to understand the risk level you and your family face at a given moment in time. This system should give a basic understanding of the situation so you and your family can be on the same page without the need for too much conversation.

There's an old saying, "Lose Lips Sink Ships" – not sure who said that but the saying is very accurate. Saying too much in today's world with electronic surveillance techniques reaching ever increasing capabilities and government's out of control invasion into our lives poses a significant security threat to those being falsely labeled as a threat or worse yet – labeled for extermination. Remember your advisory the devil walks around like a roaring lion seeking whom he may devour.

The Word of God is clear how we should handle the devil – Resist the devil and he must flee! Many of us as Christians may think the need for such as system is not necessary but what if I told you right now by doing a simply search online you can find US Government documents labeling Christians as a "Domestic Terrorist Threat". In fact Christians who are attempting to stand for truth like Pastor Chuck Baldwin or Ron Paul were put on such a list and labeled while running for President of the United States in 2008. Thereafter in 2012, we saw the IRS begin to target Christian businesses (including churches) that had or were seeking tax-exempt status – coincidence or conspiracy?

As absurd as this may sound to the uninformed Christian it is nevertheless a reality that we must face head on to have any hope of preparing properly. I encourage you to do the research for yourself, start with the MIAC Report and Project Megiddo and see just how far the rabbit hole goes. Throughout history we see the same patterns prior to Democide, Genocide, or as some would call it a Holocaust.

I would encourage every believer to check out the Voice of the Martyrs website and other sites to see how much the average Christian is being persecuted throughout the world, some I would even consider a silent holocaust as the mainstream media deliberately ignores their suffering. Very soon this will turn into a "hot war" on the Christian believer and thus the reasons for the Threat Level System as well as all our plans.

Here is a basic system and things to consider and plan for:

Threat Level System & Codes

- Green
- Amber
- Yellow
- Orange
- Red

- People involved in our network and their contact information
- Communications (How to Contact each other during an Emergency)
- Meet Up Locations
- Routes to Bug Out Locations
- Alternative Routes Home from Work

- Methods of Travel if Roads are closed (Include Maps)
- Cache Locations (with Contents Listed & Maps to them)
- Specific Assigned Roles & Duties During Emergencies
- Vital Records (Copies of Important documents, Insurance, birth records, SS Cards,
- Immigration status, Health Records, etc)
- Bug Out Bag / Go Bag
- Bug Out Vehicle
- Bug Out Information
- Mountain Retreat / Bug Out Location Information
- Bug In Information

Tactical Considerations

Tactical Considerations for the Christian who is attempting to survive a hostile situation, possibly with their family, is one of the major considerations to think about. The greatest single danger posed in any survival situation is that posed by the two-legged predators that you and I will face. As unprepared people become hungry, they will also become desperate. This will cause some to turn to criminal means to get what they need for themselves and their families.

This poses a bit of a quandary for the Christian. On one hand, we have a responsibility to provide for and protect our families. But on the other hand, we have a responsibility to feed the poor. Only in this case, feeding the poor might mean taking the food out of our own children's mouths to feed total strangers. Maybe they'll still eat today, but with limited supplies, feeding others may mean that we run out of supplies for our own family.

We are also faced with the risk of these predators attacking our families. They aren't going to listen to reason and they aren't going to be easily turned away. If we have the supplies they need, they will attack time and again, until they gain the victory.

The Bible tells us in Deuteronomy that killing in defense of home and family is acceptable. This is where the legal principle known as the "castle doctrine" came from. As long as we are killing in defense, we are okay. It is only when we attack others for personal gain, that we break God's Law. The American Christian Defense Alliance, Inc. very name indicates our defensive posture that falls in line with this Biblical principle.

So, what do we do? There are two parts of preparing ourselves in this regard. The first is making our home more defendable, by "hardening the exterior. This simply means making it harder to break into. The second part is acquiring firearms and becoming proficient in their use. Simply owning firearms isn't enough; we must learn and practice, until we reach the point where we can make Wyatt Earp himself proud.

Hardening your home means more than just putting a deadbolt on your door and locking your windows. Any criminal can kick open a dead bolted door, and glass windows are easy to break. You're going to have to go beyond the conventional wisdom if you want to keep your home safe in a time of emergency.

The weak point on your door is the door frame. So, replace the normal striker plate on the door with a security striker plate. This is a bigger striker plate, so that the force of any kick will be spread over a larger area. When you install it, use 3" screws, so that you are attaching it through the door frame and into the studs behind. That will force them to break a whole lot more than just the door frame to get the door open.

While you're at it, replace the short screws in the door's hinges with the same long screws, strengthening that side of the door as well. Replacing the standard hinges with security hinges is a good idea too, as the security hinges act somewhat like a small deadbolt, securing the hinge side of the door too.

Windows are hard to secure, but there are two options. The first is security window film. This self-adhesive film is installed on the inside of the window. It acts much like the inner layer on a windshield, preventing it from coming apart, even when broken. While it can still be broken out, that requires breaking out all the glass in the window. The other option is to put burglar bars over the windows. Custom burglar bars are better than the universal ones. Once installed, the bad guys would have to use a truck and a chain to pull them off your home and gain access – Yet another tactical consideration.

All of these tactical considerations to harden your home only delay the bad guys. Ultimately, it's up to you and your guns to protect your family. But keeping them out gives you time to react, grabbing your guns and taking a stand to fight them off.

However, tactical considerations for the Christian looking to survive a hostile situation (one in which we will be hated in all the world for Christ's name sake) should not focus so much on tactical considerations in a stationary position like your home. We must focus more on tactical considerations when Bugging Out. For more information on tactical considerations when Bugging Out please see the American Christian Defense Alliance, Inc. Book: Biblical Bug Out: Don't Bug In – Follow The Calling

Considerations for your Wife & Children

No one likes thinking about disasters and emergency situations, but the simple truth is that we are all vulnerable to them. Each year, hundreds, if not thousands of people, are affected by various natural disasters and the key to survival is preparedness.

It is especially important for women to be prepared for emergency situations. Having an emergency plan can help you remain calm, despite the circumstances, and help others that might be in need.

Women, in particular tend to be more anxious than men, which might provoke a sense of panic in case of a disaster. In the same time, women are drawn to people in need, and the key to helping those around you is preparing in advance.

The best way to prepare for a disaster is to know the proper way to respond to a variety of emergency situations. Knowing what and where the available community resources are is a great place to start – it will provide you with a sense of security, while helping you map out an emergency plan. It's often the first responders to a disaster that make the most difference, and, as a woman and wife, you are responsible not only for yourself, but for everyone around you – including spouses and children. Having an emergency kit around at all times is one of the best ways to be prepared for any sort of disaster. It should include crucial items that will aid survival, such as blankets, radio, hygiene items, as well as at least three-day supply of food and water for everyone.

Being prepared is important not only for women, but for all people. Knowing that you have an emergency plan will help you remain calm, in case there's an emergency situation, and will provide you with the opportunity to help the people around you, and make sure your loved ones are safe and protected.

Communications

Ham Radio is the most reliable form of communication for the Christian Prepper there is – Period. After extensive research I believe that the Ham Radio is simply the best form of communication for anyone truly concerned with getting through to their love ones in an emergency situation. Ham Radio gives you so many options that other forms of communication simply can't. Furthermore, Ham Radios give you outstanding range and clarity for slightly more than other radios.

Personally I wanted to go with a hand held ham radio that I could carry with me at all times, or throw it in my Bug Out Bag and be good to go. I have also invested in mobile unit for my wife and me. Both Kenwood and Yaesu put out great ham radios. We have Kenwood mobile units and Yaesu hand held units.

Now keep in mind that it is advantageous to pre-program you radios and their frequencies so you and your wife don't give out the frequency you going to - all you need to do is say go to channel 7 or whatever channel you are going to.

One thing I would caution is not to purchase a Ham Radio with a built in GPS unit. This technology while convenient today could spell disaster for you tomorrow. Having other forms of communications is a plus, but they all have their respective limitations.

Cellphones: The best cellphone to have in the event of an emergency would be from Sprint or Nextel. The phones that have the direct connect feature and are ideal in a crisis situation, as they are able to operate without the cell towers as two way radios for up to approximately 6 miles. So for an everyday carry to replace your current phone – not bad. You can add a fixed antenna to some of their phones which also increases their range. For more information check out the Sprint website. However, If you looking for privacy and security overall the older Blackberry phones are a great choice. Some

"Private" cell networks actually convert these phones even more to enhance the privacy feature already build in.

Now, yes you did just read it correctly - there are private cellphone networks - if your interested in your privacy check them out.

Now for the average person that is not tech savvy there are a few options. Some options include the following:

- CB Radios:
- FRS/GRMS
- Garmin 530:
- Satellite Phones:

CB Radios have 40 channels and is what most "Truckers" use to check out traffic and such. These are also popular for people who are into four wheeling or off road driving as well as families who enjoy camping. They are pretty straight forward to use and curtain channels are monitored by the police in the event of an emergency such as channel 9. While channel 9 is typically reserved for emergency calls channel 19 is liken to a chat room and is the channel of choice for the over the road Truckers.

Unfortunately they have only a limited range of approximately 4 miles. Additionally the communication is on the AM frequency which means the audio quality is not always the greatest. These radios do not require any special license to operate but are good for a backup nothing more.

FRS and GRMS Radios are normally sold as one radio despite being two separate bands. FRS stands for Family Radio Service. No license is require to own or operate these here in the United States and offers great voice quality. The FRS radios operate on UHF or Ultra High Frequency and are part of the FM Band. Unfortunately the draw back on these radios is the face that they have limited range. If you read on a package 20, 30, or 45 miles of operation do not believe it. You can find these in most outdoor stores or even at most electronic departments in major retailers. For the average citizen these radios have effectively replaced the old CBs or Citizen Band Radios. As a result of their overall quality and inexpensive price point many small business use these radios. Again consider these only has a backup and for no more than a mile or two away.

GRMS is short for General Mobile Radio Service. These radios are very similar to the FRS radios in just about every way but do require an FCC license to operate. The way this license works in the United States is that you complete the application and pay the fee, then you and your entire family are covered under the license. The enforcement of not completing the paperwork in unknown but if you're going to operate on these channels just fill out the paperwork to cover yourself. If you're going to purchase an FRS type radio I would recommend the Garmin walkie talkie style GPS handhelds like the 530 model.

One of the coolest things, well at least for me is the idea that I can be anywhere in the world and talk to someone I love. Satellite phones enable you to do just that. They are expense in every since of the word but if you do have the money this might be the best option for you. As there is little of a learning curve and you don't need any special license - but man oh man is it expensive. That's why for the average Christian Prepper I say Ham Radio is simply the best option, especially when bugging out.

Navigation

In today's modern world, GPS navigation has taken over from pretty much all other ways we used to navigate. But what will happen when those satellites go down? An EMP would easily take them down, rendering most of us unable to find our way much farther than back and forth to work.

It doesn't even take something as serious as an EMP to shut down our navigation. People's batteries go out all the time, leaving them without a way of using their phone and its installed GPS. While that isn't a problem if we're going back and forth to places we frequent, it can become a big problem if we have to go someplace different. It can be an even bigger problem if we're lost or a disaster has blocked our normal route.

Generally speaking, navigation requires a map and compass. The map gives you a pictorial representation of the ground you are passing over and the compass shows you which direction you're going. Assuming you can find where you are on the map, and you know which direction you're going, you should be able to find pretty much anything.

Of course, that means having a map that's appropriate for what you're doing. A common street map isn't going to help you, unless you're driving on the streets. That's typically the easiest sort of navigation, as the street signs help you to find where you are on the map.

However, once you get away from the streets, you need a topographical map. You can get these for the entire country through the U.S. Geological Survey's website. Topographical maps differ in that while they do show us streets, they are more focused on showing us the shape of the land. Their main feature is a series of squiggly brown lines, which are referred to as contour lines. These show the height above sea level for anything on the map. You can tell hills and mountain peaks, because they will be shown on the map as a series of concentric rings, even if they are lopsided ones. Those become your main landmarks for navigation in most circumstances.

If you can identify two or more terrain features (such as those mountain peaks) on your map, you can locate yourself. All you need to do is to point your compass at that peak and see what the direction, measured in degrees, is from you to it. The direction from it to you will then be that direction plus or minus 180 degrees; this is called a reciprocal bearing.

With two or more reciprocal bearings, you can draw lines (lightly, in pencil, so they can be erased) from the mountain peaks. Where those lines intersect is where you are.

To walk from where you are to where you are going you simply need to plan out your route on the map and break it down into directions that your compass can help you identify. Let's say you are going to follow a curving valley. The first direction you need to go is straight east, or 90 degrees. Then, you'll need to turn 30 degrees north to follow the valley. Okay, so you set 0 degrees directly under the needle on your compass. Then, you look for 90 degrees. That's the direction you need to go. Find a landmark in that direction and start walking towards it.

But what do you do if you don't even have a map and compass? That's where you have to rely on landmarks to help you navigate. In the Old West days, people traveled back and forth across the country, simply by following landmarks. Cowboys would sit around the campfire, describing places they've been and the landmarks to use in order to find those places. Each became a walking encyclopedia of directions to get to different places.

One trick they used, which is very valuable for us, is that of going downhill. If you're lost in the wilderness, start walking downhill. That does two things for you. First of all, it will help you find water, as water always flows downhill. Secondly, it will help you find civilization, as people tend to build roads and cities in the flatlands. As you work your way downhill, you can be assured that you are getting closer to civilization.

Fire Arms & Weapons

Firearms, one of the most controversial subjects here in America yet number two in the original Bill of Rights. The American Christian Defense Alliance, Inc. believes very strongly in the right of the people to keep and bare arms to protect themselves and their love ones. The American Christian Defense Alliance, Inc. believes that firearms of any kind are merely a tool to ensure that liberty is past down to future generations and rejects the statement that, "Guns Kill People" in full. Firearms can do nothing in and of themselves, it is the person behind the operation of the firearm that is fully responsible for any and all actions in which may cause injury of some kind.

Remember this: every time a nation has enacted a law to make firearms illegal great tyranny has risen up ... From Nazi Germany, to Communist Russia all dictators would agree gun control works. When gun control works massive amounts of people are murdered by the state. Professor John Lott has two good books about gun ownership and crime. Both of his books indicate that where there is more gun control there is more crime.

Don't let it happen again here in America. I urge all of you reading this to get prepared ASAP because the time is coming and now is when this nation will seek to take away our 2nd Amendment Right to keep and bare arms. We here at the American Christian Defense Alliance, Inc. have some suggestions regarding the purchase of firearms and recommend the following items:

AR 15 (M4 Style) piston driven with heavy barrel stamped 223/5.56 Nato. Please note that the 223 and 5.56 are not the same round and a barrel that is stamped 223 is not adequate for shooting 5.56 round, but the reverse is not true. Shoot whatever your barrel is stamped that is the bottom line. However, the heavy barrel can shoot both. This rifle is about $1,500 -2,000k.

SKS – You can find a SKS from $300-$400 in good working condition. These rifles are better then the AK 47. They have a longer heaver barrel which makes the rifle have less recoil, shoot longer and allows the person shooting to be more accurate. Plus they are piston driven.

Mini 14 (Ruger) – You can find these rifles in Walmarts or local gun shops everywhere. They cost about $600.00 and are a 223 caliber with 20 round magazines. This is considered a ranch rifle but has great multi-functions that are possible. If you are looking for a 223 caliber that is cheap this is the one, it has a great reputation for durability.

Sig Suar (9mm or 45 cal) Sig has a great reputation but the cost can be considerably more than other handguns.

Glock / Springfield XD (9mm or 45 cal) – I personally went with the XD over the Glock in 45 cal and 4" barrel. I found that through my research this weapon had everything I wanted and was less expensive then its counterparts. Best of all for those with little ones around – in the 45 cal it comes with a thumb safety. The thumb safety was the deciding factor for me. For me the 45 caliber is the ideal caliber with enough to get the job done with one shot -it is a true combat caliber.

Browning's X-Bolt Varmint Stalker – Seems to be the best bang for the buck for long-range weapons in bolt action. We recommend a 308 caliber weapon as it is the most versatile or the long range rounds. It will also be the most common round for long range snipers.

AR 15 in 308 Caliber with heavy barrel – a nice alternative for those wanting a large caliber and high mag capacity.

Self-Defense Training

As some of you may know the American Christian Defense Alliance Inc. started out as a martial arts ministry in hopes of ministering to those who would not enter a church building as well as to disciple fellow brothers and sisters in Christ in proper doctrine. Therefore, it should come as no surprise to those reading this book that the American Christian Defense Alliance highly advocates self-defense training in any preparedness planning.

Consider this, knowledge is power and the knowledge and the skill that you possess to defend you and your family could potentially be the difference maker in a life-and-death situation. Whether you're a radical Muslim terrorists or just some thug you're not going to want to deal with someone or attack someone that has the skills necessary to defend themselves in a real way.

Individuals such as thugs or radical Muslim terrorists normally attempt to attack what they perceive to be as soft targets. A soft target can be defined as a target that will offer little resistance in the process of the attacker victimizing them and offer little if any in the way of defense. This is why thugs here in America walk around in groups sometimes they are gangs other times they are not, nevertheless they attack in numbers because they are cowards. Just like radical Muslim terrorists attack soft targets such as public transportation, again which offer little if any in the way of security.

So for the Christian Prepper where does one begin - one begins first and foremost with physical fitness. I mean this with no disrespect when I say this - but if you are fat, lazy, or out of shape you are most likely incapable of doing what is necessary to defend yourself or your family from groups that attack and that my friend you will be accountable for before God. Our bodies are the temples of the Holy Spirit - The indwelling of the Spirit of God and we must respect our bodies and train them accordingly.

There are lots of ways the Christian Prepper can get in physical shape but it all starts with a mindset, the very will and determination to see things through to the end. This type of discipline is very rare in today's world especially for those that call themselves Christian.

Nevertheless, a great place to start would be to start eating right. Removing all fast food from your diet would be an excellent choice as well as eating organic foods as best as possible.

Some may argue to eliminate meat altogether from your diet. I would disagree with this as our bodies are designed to be meat eaters, however, I would limit your meat consumption to beef, chicken, lamb, fish, or rabbits – in other words try to stay away from the pork as its difficult to digest. There are plenty other options out there with wild game or in the grocery store to choose rather than ingesting pork into your body.

Water should of probably been first on the list regarding eating right. Water is the one thing on the planet that you absolutely need - yet if you look at our tap water with the fluoride and other chemicals within it, any reasonable person would conclude it's probably not a good idea to drink it. Stay away from tap water even if you purify it, filter it, or boil it – stay away. There are just too many things they are putting in the water nowadays and to be quite honest they probably don't even tell us everything that's in it.

With that in mind I would highly recommend drinking spring water that has been filtered and purified through a drip type filter.

There are several of these types of filters to choose from, each one has its pros and cons. If you're looking for a filter for everyday use within your home stick to a stainless steel model and one that has a ceramic filter. Some ceramic filters are impregnated with silver, which is an awesome thing. Silver acts as a natural antibacterial agent and keeps the actual filter as clean as possible.

The filter that I personally have is the pro-pure one. I have used the Berkey Sport model previously but did not care for the build up of slimy residue on the plastic containers. I also found that unlike the ceramic filters the carbon-based filters that are black also developed the same slimy residue. Again stick to stainless steel and ceramic filters.

Once you establish the diet that consist of higher-quality foods and remove the genetically modified foods from you and your family's life you will feel a lot healthier and begin a lifelong process learning how to eat properly.

After this established it's important to get into an exercise routine. Now for the Christian Prepper I don't recommend just any exercise routine but an exercise routine that is based on real-world application of self-defense methods. This is where we get into different styles of martial arts. Each style has different benefits to offer the end-user. However, there's only a few established styles that I know of that offer real-world self preservation techniques from a Christian perspective.

There are styles out there such as the Israeli self-defense system called Krav Maga that are established combat systems. This is a combat system with the proper mindset yet lacks Jesus Christ as its fundamental anchor and lacks the Word of God as a guiding moral principle. Now yes, this is a bit of the plug for our self-defense ministry called Seisho Ryu Goshin-Jutsu here. Our self-defense system incorporates the proper combat mindset as well as a Christian or Biblical foundation for its moral compass. I encourage each of you to find out more about our particular martial arts ministry and style by visiting our website online.

Chapter 8: Kits & Bags

If you spend any time at all around prepping or survivalist circles, you're going to end up hearing people talk about their various types of kits and bags. That's basically because of the importance of having everything you need with you to survive is so critical. While it is theoretically possible to survive without a kit, it is infinitely harder and requires much more knowledge about survival. Jesus Himself told His Disciples to go sell what you have and buy a bag . . .

Luke: 22: 35-38:
(35) And He said to them, "When I sent you without money bag, knapsack, and sandals, did you lack anything?" so they said, "Nothing." (36) Then He said to them, "But now, he who has a money bag, let him take it, and likewise a knapsack; and he who has no sword, let him sell his garment and buy one. (37) For I say to you that this which is written must still be accomplished in Me: 'And He was numbered with the transgressors. For the things concerning Me have an end." (38) So they said, "Lord, look, here are two swords." And He said to them, "It is enough."

Why is this so important? Well, Jesus Himself mentioned the need to get out and away from the city, in times of calamity. His answer was to go to the mountains. Escape and Evade is the concept . . . God says flee to the mountains and don't go back to get anything – therefore, watch and pray and be ready at all times: Matt. 24:15-20 / Mark 13

Mark 13: 14 -19 [14 "So when you see the 'abomination of desolation, spoken of by Daniel the prophet, standing where it ought not" (let the reader understand), "then let those who are in Judea flee to the mountains. 15 Let him who is on the housetop not go down into the house, nor enter to take anything out of his house. 16 And let him who is in the field not go back to get his clothes. 17 But woe to those who are pregnant and to those who are nursing babies in those days! 18 And pray that your flight may not be in winter. 19 For in those days there will be tribulation, such as has not been since the beginning of the creation which God created until this time, nor ever shall be.]

But if you're going to do that, you need to go prepared as much as possible. The problem for many people is trying to figure out what all those different bag names mean and what you actually need to have in them so you can survive. So, let's look at the various types of kits and bags you might encounter:

Survival kit - This is a small, portable kit, usually packed into something the size of a hardcover book or smaller. The idea is to have something with you at all times, that gives you the essentials for survival. Many people carry these while hiking, or keep one in their car.

EDC Bag (Everyday Carry Bag) - The EDC is intended to give you everything you would need to have with you, if a disaster happened and you were away from home. As such, it needs to cover a lot of ground in a fairly small package. A typical EDC is roughly the size of a lunch box, although the shape can vary greatly. In many cases, people add non-essential, but useful things to their EDC, such as stamps, safety pins, and a phone charger.

Get Home Bag - The idea behind a get home bag is to provide you with enough urban survival equipment and a little food, so that you can make it home from work, in the event of a disaster. The assumption is that you would have to walk, so a get home bag may even include a good pair of walking shoes. Properly done, a EDC can also be used as a get home bag.

But Out Bag (BOB) - Sometimes called a 72-hour bag, this is what you would use if you determine you need to bug out and get away from home to survive a disaster. Different people's BOB will hold different equipment, depending on their bug out plan. It is intended to get you to your survival shelter, whether that is in another city, a cabin in the woods, or if you are going to live off the land. Obviously, if you're going to live off the land, you need more survival gear.

Inch Bag - This is the extreme version of a bug out bag, for those who intend to live off the land for the rest of their lives. Inch stands for "I'm never coming back." As the name implies, that means you're going to need a lot of gear to make it through.

Regardless of the type of bag, they all have to provide for the basic survival needs, which are:

- A way to maintain your body temperature
- Clean water
- Food
- Fire
- Self-defense
- First-aid

Portability is an important consideration. You can't assume that you'll be able to use your car. Roads may be impassible, so you'll have to head out on foot. If that's the case, you want your kit or bag to be something that you can take with you. That means putting it into a portable pack, such as a backpack or over-the-shoulder bag that you can actually carry. Therefore, you also need to consider how much weight you can carry, especially in the cases of the bug out bag and inch bag.

Chapter 9: The EDC

What is an Every Day Carry (EDC)? Disasters, like babies being born, show up on when they want, not when we want. That generally means at the most inopportune times. Somethings probably not going to happen when you're at your home and have just finished repacking your bug-out bag. It'll happen when you least expect it and aren't anywhere near your survival equipment.

That's why you need to be carrying some basic things with you every single day. If you walk out your door, you need to have enough with you to make it back home. Now, that doesn't mean you need to take your bug out bag with you, but it does mean that you need some things.

The idea of Ever Day Carry (EDC) is to have the essentials with you. We can break this down into two levels; the essentials that you carry on your person and those that you carry in an EDC bag.

The difference is, there are times when you will put your EDC bag down, such as while you are at work. Most would probably leave their EDC bag in the car while working; but the items you carry on your person are those that you might need in a matter of seconds, rather than minutes.

So, what are these items that you might need in seconds?

- Pistol with extra ammo (not only to defend yourself, but to defend others; believers should take a stand to protect the weak)
- Good knife and/or multi-tool with a knife blade
- Fire starter (a butane lighter works well for this)
- Flashlight
- Cash
- Keys
- Smartphone (have survival manuals and an electronic Bible in memory)
- Tactical pen (a pen which can also be used as a hand held weapon)
- Analog watch (an analog watch can be used as a compass, a digital can't)

As you can see, these items are more focused on self-defense and getting out of your workplace, than they are anything else. The idea isn't so much allowing you to survive in the woods, or even survive sleeping in a cardboard box as you walk home from a disaster. Those items are in your Every Day Carry (EDC) kit. But there are some things that happen so quickly, that waiting till you get to your car just won't work.

If a terrorist or lunatic enters your workplace and starts shooting the place up, you don't have time to go to your car to get your gun. You need to be able to react in seconds. Likewise, if the lights go out, you'll need a flashlight on your person, not in your Every Day Carry (EDC) kit. That's the type of criteria that are used to select these items.

But it's clear that the Every Day Carry (EDC) items listed above aren't going to be enough to get you home, if you have to walk home after an EMP renders your car unusable or some other disaster happens. There are also many other things that can happen in a day, which really don't qualify as emergencies. Carrying a few basics in your Every Day Carry (EDC) to take care of those little problems is always a great idea.

Every Day Carry (EDC) bags can vary greatly in size, but for most people they're about the size of a lunch box or large fanny pack. I use an over the shoulder bag, but you can use anything. This gives me quite a bit of room for the things I feel I need.

- Shelter - 2 rescue blankets, 20' of para-cord and 10 yd of duct tape
- Rain poncho
- Lifestraw
- Nalgene water bottle
- Some high energy snacks, such as beef jerky, granola bars and nuts
- Spork - useful for those times when my lunch doesn't come with utensils
- Fire starter - I carry a lighter, as well as a BlastMatch Jr. and some WetFire cubes
- Flashlight and spare batteries
- Knife (in addition to the one in my pocket)
- Wire saw
- Compass and map - to help me find my way home
- Lock pick set (ssh!)
- Phone charger - includes cable, adapters for wall and car, as well as a charger battery
- Hair bands - useful as rubber bands for a number of things

- Emergency sewing kit - for quick repairs, heavy on safety pins
- Pen, pencil and waterproof pad
- Photocopies of my driver's license and passport
- Personal hygiene kit - includes antibacterial hand cleaner, disposable toothbrushes, deodorant, 3 compressed towels and Kleenex (can be used as toilet paper)
- First-aid - cloth bandages of various types, abdominal bandages (large bandages) alcohol wipes, cohesive medical tape, antibacterial ointment, pain relievers, antihistamine, 3 day supply of my personal medications, clotting compound and butterfly closures

With this, I have enough to get myself home from pretty much anywhere within walking distance, as well as take care of the problems which might arise during the day. If your work requires you to dress in a way that is not conducive for walking, add good walking shoes and some more comfortable clothes. Always carry a jacket with you, even on days when you don't need it. You might need it at night.

Chapter 10: The Bug Out Bag

When the time comes to bug out, you're going to need equipment and supplies to survive; that's where the bug out bag comes in. You're not going to be able to go to someplace where you can pick up a loaf of bread and a gallon of milk at the corner store. Nor are you likely to find an abandoned cabin in the woods, with a welcome sign hanging on the door.

You're going to have to live off of what you take with you, the knowledge you have and what nature provides. So, it's best to take as much with you as possible while keeping in mind weight, specifically the things that will help you survive out in the wild long-term. Of course, that means knowing how to use those things to survive with as well. Ultimately, the most important thing you can take with you is the knowledge of how to survive.

The bug out bag must provide for all of your basic needs, so it would be a good idea to review what those are. In order of priority, your needs are:

- Safety & Security
- Maintaining your body heat (this includes clothing, shelter and fire)
- Purified water
- Food
- First-aid (including personal hygiene)

Carrying all of that is going to be a bit difficult. You have to assume that you're going to have to go on foot at some point. Even if you leave home in your car or truck, chances are that you'll have to abandon it along the way. With that in mind, you need to make your bug out bag something that you can carry, such as a backpack. While other things can be used, a backpack is your best bet.

When selecting a backpack, try to avoid something that is obviously military in appearance. That's too easy to identify as what it is. You don't want people to realize that you're bugging out or recognize that you're prepared. So, you're better off with a backpacker's backpack, rather than a military one.

At the same time, if you find yourself in a combat situation prior to heading out a military backpack of some kind may not be a bad option because it is designed with combat as its primary task. You will need something rugged and durable regardless.

Also you'll want to make sure that whatever backpack you pick has a weight-bearing belt. Your legs are much stronger than your back, and can support the weight of the backpack and its contents easier than your back can. But if the pack doesn't have a belt, your back will have to carry the weight and that's a serious no, no.

Most people have to limit their pack to about one-fourth their body weight. But that's assuming that you're in shape. If not, you'll have to make it even less. One way to compensate for this is to have every member of the family carry their own pack. While women and children can't carry as big or heavy a pack as a man can, they should be able to carry their own clothes, personal toiletries and sleeping bag, as well as some of the communal food.

Bug out bags are very personal, simply because each person's situation is unique. You need to match the pack you carry to your needs, the terrain you are going to travel through, the area you are going to set up camp and your own survival skills. There's absolutely no sense in carrying equipment you can't use, no matter how useful it might seem. Additionally don't forget to leave room for weapons and ammunition – this is one of the most over looked areas of so called experts who advise on building Bug Out Bags. Safety and Security should be the number one thing to consider in your preparedness because without security you will no doubt be a victim in some way, shape, or form.

One small great option to consider for perimeter security is a 12 gage alert. This small item can be attached to a tree and loaded with a blank 12 gage round. When a person or animal walks past and trips the wire it will go off.

Now because of the nature of this device and the legality of such I have to through out a disclaimer to use according to all Federal, State, and local laws. Also please be advised that if you add any type of actual "Live Rounds" even less then lethal rounds you will be breaking some serious Federal laws – Do you own research prior to modifying this device in anyway and only use it according to its indented purpose. Now if SHTF is occurring and the United States is no longer a functional government you may want to re-evaluate things based on the current dynamics going on. Again Your Decision, Your Responsibilities, and Your possible Consequences.

Chapter 11: The INCH Bag

An INCH Bag – That Sounds Tiny . . . . What is an INCH Bag?

Most of us understand what a Bug Out Bag is unless we've been living in an isolated situation. Bug Out Bags come in all shapes and styles. Some of the commercial ones are heavy on food and water, with only a little bit of basic survival gear included. On the other end of the spectrum, we find Bug Out Bags that have every survival gadget and goodie you can imagine. This wide discrepancy raises a lot of questions in people's minds, especially people who are new to prepping.

The thing is, different people have different ideas of prepping and different ideas of bugging out. The simpler bug out bags are based on FEMA's recommended list, from their emergency preparedness website. But that list assumes that anyone bugging out is going to head for their nearest FEMA shelter to ride out the disaster. Well, I don't know about you, but turning myself over to the government is not something that I'm willing to do.

That's why my Bug Out Bag is really an INCH bag. That means "I'm Not Coming Home" bag. Does that mean that if I Bug Out, I'm never coming back? To be honest, I don't know. But I pack that bag as if that's the case, because there's no way for me to know.

You've probably seen some of those movies about the End Times, where a small group of believers is hiding out from the government and society in general. Well, what would you need, if you were in that situation? A regular bug out bag wouldn't be enough, because you would be leaving home, without the idea of ever coming back.

An INCH bag has to be heavy on survival gear, as it may very well contain all your worldly possessions, once you leave your home. If your home is destroyed and you are forced to abandon it, you could literally end up with that being everything you own. In that case, it needs to have everything you'll need while on the move.

What does that mean? It means that your INCH bag will contain enough tools and equipment that you can build a long-term shelter, start innumerable fires and filter your own water, as well as hunt and scavenge for your own food. At the same time, you're going to have to be your own doctor, provide yourself with clothing, make shoes and make anything else you're going to need. That's going to be one packed bag.

In reality, you can't fit all that in one backpack; at least, not and still be able to carry it. What you really need is more than one bag. The first one is your bug out bag, and it contains all your survival equipment. The second (and possibly third) bags will contain:

- Extra clothing
- Sleeping bags
- Ammo
- Hunting bow (with arrows)
- Seeds

Those contents are going to have to be able to help you start your homestead off in the wild. Seeds and a hunting bow are very important parts of this list, as they will give you the ability to feed yourself, without attracting attention. While a nice hunting rifle is easier to hunt with, it's also noisy. Bows may not have as long a range, but at least they're quiet.

You can build a long-term shelter with the tools you can carry in a Bug Out Bag, but it's gonna be hard. That's why I mention tools in the second bag. Those tools will be the tools you'll use to build a shelter. If you have the skills to use them consider the following tools list for specifically building a long-term shelter

Tools you may need:
- Shovel
- Full-sized axe
- Bow saw or bucksaw
- Froe (for making shingles and splitting boards)
- Adze (for squaring tops and bottoms of logs for a cabin, as well as making furniture)
- Framing chisel
- Carpenter's crosscut saw
- Pick (for breaking up ground)
- Brace & bits (for drilling holes)

I realize that sounds like a rather extensive tool list and it represents a lot of weight. But if you're going to build a log cabin out in the woods somewhere, that's the minimum you're going to need unless your just that skilled with an axe and buck saw. As it is, you're going to do a lot of backbreaking work with those tools, in order to get your cabin built. If you leave anything out, you're going to have a much harder time of it.

Chapter 12: The Bug Out Vehicle (BOV)

The Bug Out Vehicle for Christian Preppers – What's that All about? For many preppers, Bug Out vehicles are one of the "fun" parts of prepping. I mean, c'mon, who doesn't want a nice big four-wheel-drive pickup, all decked out for fun in the rocks and the mud? There's just something manly about that image, like an untamed stallion running across the prairie. We all want to be that one who catches and tames that stallion... or truck... or whatever.

But before you run out and sign a huge loan for that big truck you're wanting, let's stop and think about it for a moment. You want to be sure to get the right thing, especially on such a big purchase. New trucks are expensive, especially new four-wheel-drive trucks. Before you can even start picking out a bug out vehicle, you need to develop your bug out plan. That means knowing where you're going to go, the triggers that will tell you it's time to go and how you're going to get there. Once you have that, you're ready to start thinking about your bug out vehicle.

Some people get real elaborate with their bug out vehicles, buying or building something that's more suited for the military, than for a family. While I like those vehicles as much as the next guy, I'm not sure that they're a practical selection for a bug out vehicle. Oh, they'll get you there... at least, if the crowd of people on the freeway don't stop you and kill you for your vehicle.

You see, stealth is an important part of Bugging Out, as important as mobility. You have to assume that other people are going to be Bugging Out at the same time and that traffic will get backed up. When that happens, there's a good chance that some vehicles will run out of gas and others will overheat. Their owners will become desperate and start looking for anything they can find to help them out of the situation. In such a moment, your fancy 4×4 truck, could look like salvation to them.

The last thing you want to do is put yourself in the position where you either have to kill someone or allow them to kill you. While that may end up happening anyway, you should try and avoid it. Killing is still killing, and while the law may not be around to catch you, God's law will always be there and judge accordingly.

Of course, a lot depends on where you live. In Texas, just about everyone drives a truck or SUV. So yours won't stand out. But if you're driving that in New York, it probably will. So, pick a vehicle that will blend in and make sure it's in a color that won't attract attention.

The flip side of that coin is being able to go off-road, if you need to. There's a good chance that all those out of gas and overheated vehicles will end up blocking the highways. When that happens, it might be necessary to cut across some empty field or even some farmer's field, in order to get away. You're not going to do that successfully in your average family sedan.

Only you can analyze your escape route and determine if four-wheel-drive will really help you. If it won't then there's no real reason to buy it. You've got to balance that against your need for stealth, as well as thinking about how much space you need for your family and what you're going to take with you.

In all actuality, you probably already have a vehicle that you can use as a Bug Out vehicle. Maybe it won't be as good and maybe it won't be as sexy; but taking out a loan to buy a Bug Out vehicle, which will prevent you from doing the other prepping you need, isn't a wise use of your money. Take the time to think it through and make sure that your plan ends up fitting your budget.

Chapter 13: The Bug Out Retreat (BOR)

A Bug Out Retreat – That doesn't sound like it make sense. Preppers regularly debate the wisdom of bugging out versus bugging in, with the majority of experts coming down on the side of bugging in. But that's based on some very clear assumptions, especially the assumption that anyone bugging out is going to go live in the wild, trying to live off the land with nothing but what they're carrying in their bug out bag.

Based on that assumption, I'd have to say that bugging in is preferable. Living off the land is much harder than most of us realize. But that doesn't make bugging in an excellent idea, especially if you live in a big city. Even disasters as small as a hurricane can cause a breakdown in society, at least to some extent. If that's the case, then what's going to happen with a major disaster? Say, something nationwide? The lawless element of society will grow and they'll be attacking anyone they can, in order to find the things that they need to have in order to survive. Being a prepper around such people will become very dangerous.

That's why a bug out retreat is a superior option to bugging in. A bug out retreat gives you the option of leaving town and getting away from the two-legged predators, without having to put your family at risk. By pre-planning and preparing someplace to go, you can best protect your family. But there's another reason for us to bug out, rather than bug in. That is, Jesus gave us that advice. In fact, He tells us that in three of the gospels (Mt 24:16; Mar 13:14; Luke 21:21), which means it must be important. Specifically, he tells us to go to the mountains when we see the abomination of desolation. So, where are there mountains nearby you?

Hold on, I can already hear you. There are some of you out there saying that you can't afford a bug out retreat. Maybe that's true or maybe you're just thinking of it the wrong way. Buying the land is usually the most expensive part. If you can get away from that part, you can take out a lot of the cost of building your bug out retreat. In fact, that opens a number of possibilities to you.

The first of these is to create it on property owned by a friend or family member who lives out of town. Perhaps their reason for living outside of town is that they want to survive. If that's the case, you can form a survival team together. Then, you can build a shelter on their property out of scavenged materials. Another option is to use a travel trailer. You can buy older used travel trailers for a couple thousand dollars. If you're the do-it-yourselfer type, you can fix that trailer up, making a nice shelter out of it. Then you either keep it at home or find a good place to store it, that would be conveniently close to where you plan on placing your bug out shelter.

Don't forget small towns either. Most of them will be much safer during a crisis than the big cities. But people who live in small towns will probably be suspicious of strangers. So, you will need to integrate yourself with that town beforehand, so that they accept you when you arrive. Regardless of the type of bug out retreat you create, the mountains are the best place to do it. Not only will you be well hidden from those two-legged predators, but the mountains provide an abundance of resources which you will need to have access to, in order to survive.

Chapter 14: Caching

Caches? What in the World are Caches; is that like a peanut? No, No that a Cashew. If you are still reading at Chapter 14 you may know what Caches are, but how much do you really know? One common mistake for Preppers to make is to keep their entire stockpile in their home, in one location or in one cache. On one hand, that makes sense, as most people plan on bugging in during a disaster, rather than bugging out.

But on the other hand, having everything in your home or one location means that in the case of a disaster that destroys your home, or in the case of a mob attacking your stockpiled location, you lose everything you have – And the wife is not going to like that one bit, especially when she most likely put up with your crazy prepping for so long. Now when it's needed the most it's not there – Yea, definitely not going to go over well.

That's why supply caches are so important. They spread your supplies around, putting them in convenient places where you might need them. That way, no matter what you end up having to do to survive a disaster, you have some supplies readily at hand. Now these supplies will not be very extensive most likely but will give you what you need to hand on and survive.

To accomplish this, you need caches in multiple locations. While that is more work, it will ultimately serve you better to have several different caches which you can access, rather than just one – And the wife can be happy. Basically, you want to break your caches down into a few basic areas:

Near your home – If you are bugging in, you want extra supplies that you can access readily. These caches also serve if your home is broken into and your supplies are stolen or your home is destroyed and you need some ready supplies. Local storage units are great for this – But think Creatively

Your workplace – If you own your own business or you have some storage space available at your work, you could create a small cache there. That would provide you with supplies for yourself and your co-workers, if a disaster leaves you trapped at work for a few days.

Your bug-out location – This is probably the most important place to have caches prepared. You probably won't be able to take everything you need with you, so by having caches at or near your bug out location, you ensure that you will have supplies available. If you own that location, you can stock it well, but if not, you'll need to find someplace to hide your caches.

Along your bug out route – The average bug out bag only has three to five days worth of food in it. But if you have to go on foot, you may need many more days to get to your survival retreat than the food you are carrying. Putting a couple of caches along the way allows you to re-supply. You should do this every 3-5 Miles, especially if you're traveling with children.

Combat Caches – This is something you should consider wisely and as I must mention in accordance with all local, state, and federal laws. Combat Caches are designed to give you a tactical advantage and could be stocked with a multitude of items that include things like sealed ammo, parts to firearms, knives, etc. – Just use your imagination but stay within the law. Combat Caches should be placed in a tactically advantageous location such as high ground, rocky terrain, vantage points, etc.

Cashes . . . Closing Remarks

As you can see, properly placing a cache requires considerable forethought. You need to pick locations that are going to work out well as part of your overall survival plan. Not just anyplace will do. But where do you actually make the cache?

One of the best locations I've run across for a survival cache is a rented storage locker; the kind that has sprung up all across the country as people's possessions outgrew their storage space. You can rent small spaces the size of a closet, for a minimal monthly fee, which is enough space to set up a pretty good cache.

Another option is to establish one at the home of a like-minded friend or family member, if they have space. Of course, they'll have to be someone you can trust.

The other possibility is to bury your caches. This is best for the ones along your bug out route and may also be best at your bug out location. Plastic five-gallon buckets work well for this, as they are water-tight, can hold a fair amount and are readily available at all home improvement centers. You can also use PVC pipe, but that won't hold as much.

If you bury caches, make sure that you have multiple landmarks to locate them by. Don't use trees for landmarks, as they can burn down or be cut down. Instead, use features of the landscape, such as rock outcroppings. Those are permanent, short of removing them with heavy equipment or dynamite. If that becomes the case, you'll probably lose your cache anyway.

You can put literally anything in a cache, but the basic idea is to use them for food, ammunition and basic survival equipment.

You should already have your survival equipment with you, so the only reason I'm mentioning survival equipment is in case you lose yours or can't get to your bug out bag. Other than that, the biggest item is food, as that's what you'll be consuming the most of.

Chapter 15: Alternative Housing Options

Now there are two options – Stay put and dig in or Bug Out. As we already clarified in a previous chapter God's plan is for us to Bug Out so we can avoid being a victim of circumstances. Have you ever realized that God always provides a way of escape for His people, whether it's an Ark, Rapture, or Mighty Man of God to lead His people – He always provides a way of escape.

Tiny Houses may seem to be the next Big Thing but are they right for the Christian Prepper? Tiny Houses offer a lot of options but they are still stationary. I don't consider the Tiny Houses on Trailers actually Tiny Houses. When I talk about Tiny Houses I'm talking about a small shed like building that is on the ground – just so we are on the same page here. It makes sense why so many people considering them.

Many are sick of the rat race and are actively taking steps to ensure their future survival both economically and beyond. It is absolutely possible to have a Tiny House built for 10-20k that has enough room for you and your family's needs.

If you put it on some land . . . . you're good to go. For some that might make a good Bug Out Retreat. Others might consider this option if they have special needs or situations such as an ill family member. However, if at all possible actively consider a mobile lifestyle – This is the Biblical example.

RVing Full-Time may be the way to go. I gotta say hitting the open road and not looking back does sound very appealing right now with the way our country is. I actually believe that the American Christian who can do RVing full-time should do so. I believe God calls us to use "Escape & Evasion" tactics in these last day when we will be hunted and killed in the 5th Seal. Start the process today.

Chapter 16: Alternative Energy Options

Alternative Energy Options for the Christian Prepper . . . Do we really need to worry about Alternative Energy Options as a Christian while Bugging Out? However, what if we're not on the Bugging Out and like most experience a power outage do to a storm or disaster that wasn't expected? We have to plan for multiple scenarios at the same time to truly be prepared. It's not all just about the End of Days. Let's think about a few things . . .

In pretty much any disaster, there's one thing in common; a loss of electrical power. In fact, it doesn't even take a true disaster to cause a power outage. A spring thunderstorm or a buildup of ice in the winter can bring down power lines, leaving people without power.

Our electrical grid is aging. Some parts are over 100 years old. But it was only designed to last 50 years. So, it's not surprising that winter storms and more serious disasters can all cause serious problems with the grid.

But with modern society's dependence upon electricity for almost everything, this loss of power can have grave consequences, especially if it takes more than a few hours to restore.

The only security any of us can have against the loss of power is being able to generate our own. Even limited electrical generation capability, while not enough to operate everything in our homes, will allow us to operate some critical systems, keeping our food from spoiling, maintaining communications, operating the many small electronics we use every day, providing ourselves with light and operating medical equipment that family members might need. While there are many different ways of generating electrical power, there are really only three that are practical for most people to use. Others are either too expensive or require special circumstances, such as a private river to erect a water wheel. For most these three are sufficient:

Gas Generator – While the most common means of producing electrical power in an emergency, gas generators are actually the least efficient.

The high cost of fuel to operate the generator quickly overcomes the savings in buying the equipment. However, if one has a limited budget to spend on electrical generation, a gas generator is the least expensive to buy.

Solar Panels – Solar has become the "go to" method for home power generation. Sunlight is a plentiful resource in most of the country, so there is no shortage of fuel to power the system. However, it is the most expensive to buy and install. You can mitigate this cost by building your own, saving about half the price of commercially manufactured systems. The cost of the system is also offset by the fact that it has zero operating cost.

Wind Turbine – Wind power has become a popular alternative for green energy companies. It is cheaper to build than solar and produces more power. However, wind only produces electricity when you have winds that are over ten miles per hour. So, it doesn't work well in all parts of the country. Like solar, you can save a considerable amount of money building your own.

The best is to integrate systems, together, such as having some solar and a wind turbine. That way, there is power being produced, regardless of the weather.

A fully integrated system should also have a battery bank, with the solar panels and wind turbine charging the batteries and power being drawn off the batteries to power the electronic devices needed in the home. While a fairly hefty additional cost, this ensures that there is always electrical power available in the home.

When looking at alternative power systems for use in an emergency, keep in mind that it isn't necessary to create enough electricity to power everything in your home. All you need is enough for your essential systems, such as those mentioned above. Creating a system that powers your whole home or RV needs is inherently expensive. If you would like more information on Alternative Energy Options check out some of the links below.

Alternative Energy Options for the Christian Prepper:

- Sun Jack
- Renology
- Goal Zero

Chapter 17: What to Buy
A Basic Shopping List for Your BOB

Basic Tools for your Bug out Bag: Concept: Never rely completely on one particular item to get a job done!

- Back Pack
- Your Weapons & Ammo (a Ruger 10/22 or Shotgun is a Great Choice for general survival but will only help a little when dealing with the two legged bad guys – for that consider the AR15, AK, or SKS.
- Good Knife (The Best You Can Afford)
- Multi-Function Tool (Gerber or Leatherman)
- Folding Saw (Bahco Laplander)
- Bob's Quick Buck Saw (with extra blades)
- One Gransfors Bruks Axe
- Cold Steel Special Forces Shovel
- 550 Cord 300 feet and number 12 Bank Line (1lb spoil)

Shelter:

- Small 2 person Tent. This is actually a one-person tent with your gear. If you have a family plan accordingly. However, just remember to stay out of sight. Reusable Space Emergency Blanket / Tarp
- SOL Emergency Bivy – Green
- United States Military Bivy is another option. This is more durable but add a little more weight.
- One 100% Wool Blanket. Make sure it's actually 100% wool.

Fire Starting Equipment:

- Faro Rod
- Magnifying Glass
- Flint & Steel
- Metal Container holding Card Cloth
- Magnesium Block
- Matches in water proof container of some kind
- Lighters
- Cotton Balls covered in petroleum jelly
- Knowledge and Ability to start fire using primitive techniques such as the bow and drill & hand drill and Modern Techniques of using Batteries to start fires.

Food:

- Cliff Bars (20 grams of Protein each)
- Organic Trail Mix
- 1 Mainstay Food Ration Bar (3600 cal.)
- 3-5 MREs (because you don't need water to cook them)
- Snares, Fishing Yo Yos, and two 220 Conibear Traps
- The Ability to catch, trap, or hunt game to secure a renewable food source as well as process it in the field. Don't forget to bring some zip lock bags. Learn how to smoke you meats to help preserve it.

Water:

- Purification Tablets
- Water Filter (Katadyn Pocket Micro filter)
- 1 Plastic fold-down 5 gallon water container
- 1 Steel cup/bowl for boiling water (Stanley put out a really good little kit)
- Knowledge and Ability to gather and create safe drinking water through creating a Solar Still, Survival Filter, and Boiling Water

Documents:

- Small Bible
- Small copy of Declaration of Independence and US Constitution with Bill of Rights
- Small survival field book
- And of course maps of locations you will be traveling in.

Chapter 18: Personal Care

In chapter 7 I briefly discussed proper food and water, in this chapter we will cover personal care as it relates to bugging out. Additionally we will cover hygiene while bugging out and medical training you should receive prior to having to bug out.

Hygiene and Personal Care

Hygiene and personal care while bugging out is something of critical importance. Hygiene and personal care is the number one issue taking people out worldwide. Even more than war improper hygiene and personal care is one of the fastest ways to take you and your family out of the game. Therefore it's important to plan and prep accordingly. Those with special needs should take great care and caution in the planning as medications and urgent care most likely will not be available. There are options to stock up on antibiotics if that's something you are in need of through the use of fish antibiotics. However, use at your own discretion and accordingly to all applicable laws.

The label itself will tell you this is only for fish. A great Christian Prepper who just also happens to be a nurse did a great video on this a while back just search out the Patriot Nurse on YouTube. She does a lot of great videos on medical preparedness and does offer classes throughout the country. If you do stop by and visit her let her know you found her through our book.

One of the main things to throw into your bug out bag is a personal care kit. This kit should include things such as tweezers, toenail clippers, a pair of scissors, a bandanna and other individual specific hygiene items. Again remember stores are not open so what you have is what you have and you need to be able to improvise with what you bring. Women especially should take note of this and plan accordingly to deal with her menstrual cycle.

Medical Training

At the bare minimum every adult should be trained in First Aid and CPR. Medical training should be completed prior to any situation taking place if at all possible.

Do not put off medical training, as you do not know when a situation will take place in which you may need this particular training. I personally am an American Red Cross Instructor and have taught numerous individuals first aid and CPR classes at different places I've worked. I continue to offer training to those within our organization.

This training is on a first-come first serve basis and is limited to 10 people per class. In the future the American Christian defense Alliance, Inc. hopes to offer further courses from the American Red Cross. Their training is top-notch and very professional.

Conclusion

The conclusion of this book is actually the beginning of your journey. Now is the time to take massive action and get things done again not out of the spirit of fear, but out of the spirit of love using your sound mind that God has given you. We will all go through different spurts and times in which we feel anxious, worried or fearful and these are the times that try men's souls - yet as you cling ever closer to Christ and His word you will have the peace of God that surpasses all understanding for God cannot lie when he promises in His Word is an unstoppable truth.

We have covered a lot of subjects throughout this book yet to be quite honest we've only scratched the surface. I hope that you use this book as it's intended, for the purpose of this book is for you and your family to get prepared as best as possible from a Christian perspective, to give you the operational framework that is necessary instead of going through all of the craziness to put the pieces of the puzzle together – I hope in some small way this helps put the pieces of the puzzle together that much quicker for you and that you truly gain the necessary understanding that God wants for you. For God does not desire for His people to be ignorant – what does the word of God say, my people perish for lack of knowledge. God doesn't want His people to perish but to have an intimate personal relationship with Him through understanding the Word of God.

I hope you will also pass on this book to potentially a nonbeliever in Jesus Christ who may be receptive to information regarding prepping and preparedness – again our greatest prep, our greatest asset if you would in our life should be Jesus Christ and even now I still implore you to come to Jesus right now while you yet still can, while there is still hope for change in Christ Jesus, while you yet still have breath in your lungs to speak the words that can bring everlasting healing, hope, peace, and everlasting life – do it now my friend. For God said in an acceptable time I've heard your cry and helped you - behold now is the time for salvation, behold now is the time.

This is the American Christian Defense Alliance, Inc. attempt to help warn and prepare you before it's too late – We have done our part, Now what will you do?

Special Gift

God has a Gift for You!   The Plan of Salvation:

There is no formal î prayer of salvation as many churches would have you believe, God's Word is very clear - there is only one way to get to the Father in heaven and that is through Jesus Christ (John 14:6). Jesus says that you must be born again to enter into heaven (John 3:3-5).

Salvation is simply the first step in building an open and honest relationship with God. We all have sinned and fall short every day, but there is Hope in Jesus Christ - Just cry out to God in sincerity and honesty asking for forgiveness and for Him to Save you, Sanctify you, and fill you with His Holy Spirit - Ask for His will to be done in your life on earth as it is in Heaven and That's it, now just keep it real with God.

A Warning:

The Christian walk is not an easy life on the surface. The Word of God says that we will be hated in all the world for Christ namesake (Matt. 24:9). The Bible says that in the last days are enemy prevail against us physically until Christ returns to save us (Dan 7:21, 22). Furthermore, we must endure hardship as a good soldier of Jesus Christ (2 Tim 2:3) and yet we are never alone in this, God promises us that He will never leave us nor forsake us if we believe in him (Matt.28:20).

In everything we go through we have the peace and joy of God which surpasses all understanding (Philp. 4:6-8) The Bible declares, "For I consider the sufferings of this present time are not worthy to be compared with the glory which shall be revealed in us". (Rom 8:18). However, in all these things we are more than conquerors through Jesus Christ (Rom. 8:37)

Stay In Contact

Our Contact Information

Stay in Contact with the American Christian Defense Alliance, Inc. Contactus@acdainc.org Or Email Us Though Our Website At: www.ACDAInc.Org

Join Our Mailing List

We also Greatly Appreciate You Signing Up For Our Mailing List and Providing a Good Rating and review for this Book. Your reviews help other people like yourself find this book on Amazon and benefit from its contents.

If You or Your Family have been Blessed by this book please let us know by dropping us a line through our website at http://acdainc.org

Thanks Again for Reading

God Bless!

Find All Our Books On Amazon

Our Books on Amazon:

Real Men Don't Make Promises: Understanding Oaths, Pacts, Covenants & Promises From A Biblical Perspective

Salvation for Your Unsaved Mom: 10 Things to Tell Your Mom Before She Dies

God's Super Minions: Living Faithfully and Obediently in God

The Perfection of Purity: A Message To My Daughter

A Vague Notion: How To Overcome Limiting Beliefs of Fear and Anxiety Through the Word of God

God's Green Smoothie Book: The Naked Truth

Biblical Bug Out: Don't Bug In - Follow The Calling

Christian Prepping 101: How To Start Prepping

Dirt on Your Tabies: 7 Short Stories of Seisho Ryu Ninjutsu